Our

Journey

Past, Present, future

THE BLACK SHIELD POLICE ASSOCIATION

Our Journey Past, Present, Future © 2016 by the Black Shield Police Association.

This book is a work of non-fiction.

For information contact: info@uptownmediaventures.com
Book and Cover design by Team Uptown

http://uptownmediaventures.com

ISBN: 978-1-68121-051-3

First Edition: October 2016

Edited by Cheryl Johnson and K Kelly McElroy

10 9 8 7 6 5 4 3 2 1

DEDICATION

Our Journey Past, Present, Future

Is dedicated to all the dedicated officers of color who selflessly served the City of Cleveland, Ohio and to the entire community of the City of Cleveland and to all of the supporters of the Black Shield Police Association

The Black Shield Police Association Headquarters, 2016

Our Journey

Past, Preset, Future

is a concise summary of the history and goals of the Black Shield Police Association. We have come a long way, but greater accomplishments are ahead!

INTRODUCTION

Our Journey Past, Present, Future kicks off the Black Shield Police Association's OurStory Initiative. We are compiling the personal accounts and experiences of many of our members, whether they be retired or still serving. The results of the interviews and research will be presented in a major publication that will be available to the community-at-large, as well as the members of the Black Shield Police Association, as a historical reference.

Of course, all of the Black Shield's other initiatives, like minority police recruitment, are still ongoing and the fight for civil justice and equality are on-going.

It is hoped that you enjoy the messages and the spirit of intent that this publication is seeking to convey.

The Black Shield

Police Association

Lynn Hampton with Winston Gragg, CEO of the Cleveland Chapter of Infinite Scholars at the African American Music Association's Scholarship Week College Fair at the MLK Branch of the Cleveland Public Library

STATEMENT BY BLACK SHIELD PRESIDENT

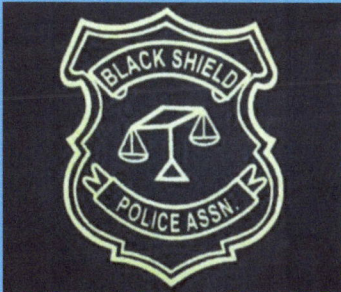

The Black Shield Police Association

"Community Policing is great, however Conscious Policing is required."

I am pleased and humbled to serve my fellow officers. My goal is to empower the entire community by ensuring that the community-at-large is appropriately represented in the Cleveland Police force.

Of course the campaign to successfully recruit minority candidates to the Cleveland Police department continues, along with increased vocalization against social injustice by certain elements in police departments throughout the United States.

Lastly, we are embarking on a major effort to document to history of minorities in the Cleveland Police Department.

Please join me as we successfully achieve our goals!

Lynn Hampton speaking at the African American Music Associations Scholarship Banquet during the Infinite Scholarship Week at the Tudor Arms Hotel

HISTORICAL OVERVIEW

The Black Shield

Police Association

In 1945, a small group of Black police officers that included two female officers, Betty Anthony and Ione Kenny Biggs, met at the home of a probation officer, John Jones. The group met to discuss the unfair treatment of Black officers in the Cleveland Police Department. The group realized that "In Unity, There is Strength." In March of 1946, the Shield Club was formed. This was a turning point for Blacks on the Department. There were other organizations but Blacks were not allowed to join. Due to this fact, Black officers were compelled to form the Shield Club as a social club entity.

Members during the formative years included David Beasley (the first president), Edward Coleman (vice - president), Harrison McCorkle (treasurer), Lynn Coleman (secretary), Thomas Hill, Warren Brown, Robert Garner, Betty Anthony, Inone Kenny Biggs, John Jones, Claude Lee, George Ballard, Edward Mitchell, Charles Reynolds, and Pete Duff.

The principle benefit of the Shield Club was to assist Black officers to maintain and strengthen self-esteem within an atmosphere of indifference. In 1969, the Shield Club was charted as a non-profit organization and was the third oldest Black police Organization in the country.

In August, the National Black Police Association was founded representing more than 40,000 minority officers in the United States and England. In the year 2000, the National Black Police Association became international with members in the United Kingdom, Canada, and the Bahamas.

In 1972, the Shield Club filed a lawsuit against the City of Cleveland for discrimination against minorities. After several years of discovery and litigation, the U.S. District Court approved a consent decree. The consent decree established many procedures to affect a prospective remedy to eliminate race discrimination in the City of Cleveland Division of Police. Fred Johnson, as president, often spoke out against the unfair treatment of minorities on the Department and the citizens of Cleveland. His job was always in jeopardy, but he continued to fight for what was right.

Jean Clayton, who is remembered and honored as the "Mother of the Black Shield Police Association," joined the Cleveland Police Department in 1951. She joined the Shield Club and worked to make the police department more responsive to the needs of its Black citizens. She successfully sued the City of Cleveland and the police department on behalf of women who were discriminated against with respect to all aspects of transfers, assignments, promotions, and classifications.

In 1978, the Shield Club became the Black Shield Police Association. The generous labors of its members improved the work conditions in the Department. The Black Shield Police Association supports the philosophy of community policing which calls for a true and cooperative partnership between the community and the police for safer communities. The Black Shield Police Association is generous in making donations to charities such as the United Negro College Fund, shelters, food basket programs, etc. Over $25,000 has been donated in scholarships to students seeking higher education. We believe "It Takes a Village to raise a Child."

In December 1995, history was made when the top two positions were won by women. Francine Eppinger became the first female president and Hughlean Medlea became the first vice-president.

A LOOK BACK

THE ANTHONY JOHNSON SCHOLARSHIP AWARD DINNER DANCE OCTOBER 24, 2015

The Black Shield

Police Association

Program Processional
Presentation of Color Guards,
Cleveland Police Honor Guards

Invocation
Reverend Otmous Howard, BSPA Chaplain

National Anthem
Antionette Black

Introduction of the Master of Ceremony
Michael Belle, 1st Vice President

Introduction of Dias
Harry Boomer, Master of Ceremony

Dinner Welcome
Lynn Hampton, President

Keynote Address
Former State Senator Nina Turner

Awards Presentation
Lynn Hampton, Michael Belle

Retiree's and Promotional Presentations
Harry Boomer, Lynn Hampton,
Michael Belle, Juanita Black

Scholarship Presentations
(Anthony Johnson, Jean Clayton and Fred
Johnson) Juanita Black, CPD (ret.), Tracy
Johnson, Ericka Owens

N.O.B.L.E.S. Scholarship Presentation
Carolyn Williams

Remarks
Juanita Black, Program Chairman

Benediction
Rev. Otmous Howard

FEATURE STORY

A DISCUSSION WITH FRED JOHNSON

The Black Shield Police Association

B lack Shield Police Association (BSPA) president Lynn Hampton expressed a desire to create a compilation of the experiences of various Black police officers. He expressed particular interest in honoring the men and women who paved the way for current police officers in Cleveland, Ohio.

I told him that we can publish an introductory book to inform the BSPA membership of the organization's initiative. Hampton instructed that he wanted "Fred Johnson to be interviewed." He cautioned me to obtain not just a summary of his achievements, but to delve into the person and, "mind set" of the former BSPA president who retired from the Cleveland Police Department in 1983.

Hampton gave me Mr. Johnson's contact information and I was able to arrange a meeting with him. While he initially seemed a little hesitant when I told him that I wanted to interview him regarding his experience as a Cleveland police officer, Mr. Johnson did agree to meet with me in his home the next day.

After my interview with Mr. Johnson and his family, it became apparent just how much this man went through in his fight for the rights of Black police officers and the Black community in Cleveland.

The Noblest of Intentions

I began the interview by asking Mr. Johnson what prompted him to join the police department. His response was very straight-forward. "I thought I would make more money than I was making if I worked as a police officer. And I also wanted to make a difference in the community because Blacks were treated very poorly by the police back then in the late 60s and early 70s."

Mr. Johnson attended John Hay High School and recalled trying out for the baseball team. He was told by one of the coaches that Blacks were not allowed to play baseball and was urged to try out for football or basketball.

It is interesting to note that this occurred around the same time that Jackie Robinson was brought to the Brooklyn Dodgers, ushering in the integration of major league baseball. This may not have ultimately been in the

best interest of Blacks, especially considering the subsequent demise of the Negro Leagues - but that is another story.

Mr. Johnson's inclination to serve the community did not surface early on in his career. "I sometimes think I should have got involved in the struggle sooner, but I gave myself the excuse that I had a family and needed to take care of them. Of course, this is why many Black police officers don't unite and join in the struggle today. But, eventually, I just had to do something."

In any event, Mr. Johnson exerted a valiant effort despite the obstacles and indignities that police officers of color had to endure in those days. He rose above many slights and abuses from supervising officers on the way to becoming a role model for fellow officers.

The Life and Times of Officers of Color

Mr. Johnson seemed to light-heartedly reminisce about some of the racially charged incidents that he and other officers of color experienced from their white counterparts on the force. He does not seem bitter. Rather, he appears to be at peace with the contributions he has made confronting injustices, encouraging unity among the ranks, and obtaining successful results during his tenure.

The Challenges of Getting Hired

Mr. Johnson recalled the racist hiring (or not hiring) tactics used by the Cleveland Police Department during his early days on the force. "The powers that be would only select blacks who they thought would go along with the system. They would not hire very educated Blacks or Blacks who were otherwise highly qualified. They had a fear that very intelligent Blacks would cause too many problems and disrupt their well-oiled system of institutional racism."

Another scenario recalled by Mr. Johnson, involved a Black candidate who was otherwise qualified, but was not hired due to some alleged mental health or physical limitation. The candidate informed a local councilperson who referred the candidate to Dr. Crile, a doctor of great repute and one of the founders of the Cleveland Clinic. Dr. Crile determined that the candidate was in very sound mental and physical health, compelling the Cleveland Police Department to hire him. "Of course, there were many such occurrences," said Johnson.

Reflections of Police and Community Racism

"Black police, in those days, never policed on the West side of Cleveland. One day, me and my partner decided to venture off into the West side of town. We were immediately confronted with questions from folks in that area as to why we were there," said Johnson. They decided to go back to the East side of town.

"I was eventually assigned to the First District on the Westside, working in and around the West 130th and Bellaire neighborhood area for a short time. I was told by my superiors that they had to 'keep an eye' on me," Johnson laughed.

Mr. Johnson chuckled when giving an account of responding to a call from the owner of a bar on East 93rd Street reporting a shooting. Upon seeing Mr. Johnson and his partner, dressed as plain-clothed detectives, the bar owner called the Department back stating, "You sent the wrong ones!"

"Me and my partner were often told by business owners, when we wanted to get food and such, that they did not sell to Blacks or 'Negros' as we were called back then." I asked him how did this make him feel and how did he react to such blatant racism. "We had to look at the big picture and often simply turned around and walked away. We had bigger fish to fry."

Lastly, Mr. Johnson accounted a scenario where a Black officer, Mr. Lynn Coleman, was instructed by a superior officer to not leave the confines of a square box he drew in chalk on the ground unless "nature called." Coleman was Johnson's best friend and Johnson hated having to watch his dear friend endure such humiliation.

"Even if a person of color did get hired by the Cleveland Police Department, they had little or no chance to get promoted and this was a serious problem that started getting me into a more activist mindset."

The Commitment

"After a while I just had to get involved, along with other seriously committed people from all over the country. Here in Cleveland, we did not get total support from the Black police officers, but we got enough and we started addressing issues that concerned our communities," said Johnson.

Mr. Lynn Coleman was a very strong influence upon Mr. Johnson during these years. "So I decided to get involved and push ahead with our agenda. There was no looking back after that point – no excuses."

The BSPA was at the forefront of police activism – a model that was replicated by many Black police organizations over the years. In 1972, the Shield Club was established as a non-profit organization and later that year, the National Black Police Association (NBPA) was established representing more than 40,000 Black officers across the United States. In 2000, the NBPA went international with members in the United Kingdom, Canada, and the Bahamas.

"In establishing the NBPA, we interacted with Black police associations from all over the country including Chicago, Pittsburgh, New York City, Akron, Youngstown, Cincinnati, Detroit, along with other cities," said Mr. Johnson.

Mr. Johnson noted, "People like Renault Robinson and Howard Saffold from Chicago really sacrificed a great deal for our cause and I am very grateful for their contributions."

In 1972, the Shield Club filed a lawsuit against the City of Cleveland for discrimination against minorities. This was just the beginning...

The Challenges

"Among the challenges we encountered was maintaining unity among the ranks so that we could pursue our goals as a united front. We never did get full Black participation, but we did get enough," said Johnson.

I asked him what level of cooperation or lack thereof he got from politicians, the police department, and/or other community leaders. Johnson responded, "We got absolutely no cooperation from the Cleveland Police Department and the politicians were not too much better. Institutional racism was so ingrained in the Department that they really acted as if they were not doing anything wrong. We only accomplished our goal because of the unity we had at that time."

Johnson added, "Of course, as a detective I was privileged and happy to be able to give the lawyers the necessary information and evidence they need to successfully litigate the civil rights action in 1972."

After the successful civil rights action resulting in the consent decree, Mr. Johnson witnessed the following inscription on a bathroom wall in the basement of the Central Police station:

"Conduct your job with vigor or you might be replaced by a nigger."

"That's just the way it was," said Johnson matter-of-factly.

It is evident that despite such obstacles and challenges, Fred Johnson continues to be at peace with himself and that he is blessed to be where he is now. More on that later...

The Triumphs

Fred Johnson eventually became president of the Shield Club and was propelled into the spotlight, due to his commitment to the cause and tireless work. The work on the civil rights lawsuit against the City of Cleveland continued for several more years.

In the meantime, the cause became a family affair. "When we were children, my sister Charmainne and I were always doing something to assist our dad in the cause. The production of the monthly newsletter was a family endeavor. We collated, folded and stamped each one. We witnessed, first-hand, the struggle and the challenges," said daughter Cheryl Johnson.

MEMBER OF THE YEAR

Presented To

Fred Johnson

For His Outstanding
And Loyal Services
Which Continue To Enhance
The Goals Of The
Black Shield Police Association

October 3, 1992

"Ultimately, we did start to usher in changes when we won a favorable determination by Judge Thomas in 1974 and eventually obtained a consent decree with the City. Our success was noted by Black police associations all over the country," said Johnson. Judge Thomas found the City of Cleveland guilty and imposed an 18% set-aside for minorities.

"These activities fostered an era where Blacks could get promotions within the Department and we saw a lot of positive results from the activism during those days," said Johnson.

Per a consent decree, a hiring quota was established that mandated initially 18% minority representation and ultimately increased to 43% minority representation.

Behind Every Good Man

Mrs. Anna Marie Johnson is a retired educator, who taught elementary education for 30 years in the Cleveland Public Schools. She was a stronghold and bedrock for Mr. Johnson during those tumultuous years of activism. She maintains that quiet fire to this day.

In my discussion with Mrs. Johnson, apart from Mr. Johnson and their daughter, Mrs. Johnson gave me the most concise encyclopedic rendition of Mr. Johnson's accomplishments. She's witty and sharp as a tack!

Mrs. Johnson, the matriarch of the Johnson family, certainly is a beautiful person inside and out as verified by Johnson himself. "I simply cherish her and would not know what to do without her," said Mr. Johnson.

During my interview with Mr. Johnson, Mrs. Johnson would supply details, as if on cue, when Mr. Johnson did not give the complete account. I would look at Mr. Johnson and he would have a half-smile, with that knowing look on his face – that made me smile.

Mrs. Johnson displayed a quiet yet extremely strong inner presence that manifested itself with class and intelligence. It should not be any wonder that the couple celebrates over 60 years of marriage.

The Struggle Continues

As pointed out by Johnson's daughter Cheryl, "Affirmative action is now effectively illegal, and we need to establish a revamped agenda to address the backlash which continues to reinforce systematic racism."

"A big issue then is a big issue now – the use of deadly force by the police in the Black community," said Johnson. "Community unity is necessary more than ever

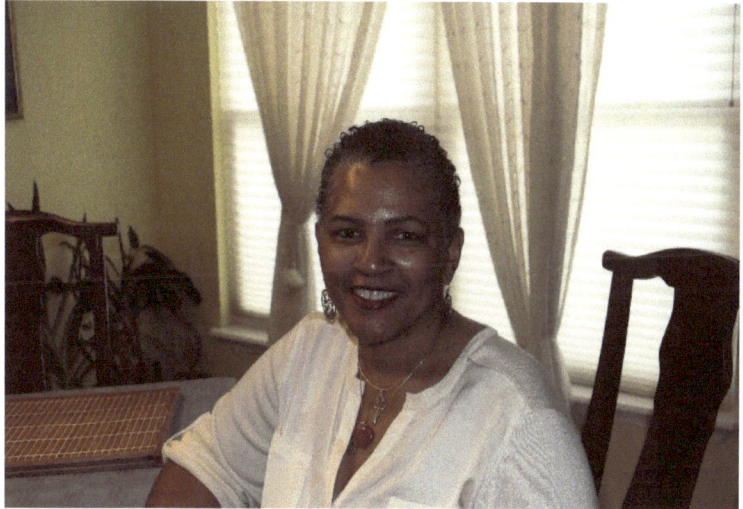

by people of all walks of life because that old blatant racist system is rearing its ugly head again."

"For the National FOP and the local CPPA to feel comfortable enough to endorse such a divisive person as Trump is clear evidence that the racial climate has not really improved," says Cheryl Johnson.

I asked Mr. Johnson to give some admonition to the present and future activists in our communities.

"We must always look at the big picture instead of just looking at our own individual circumstances. We must always be good citizens, yet never be scared to speak out. I am a little disappointed that more Black people aren't vocal – especially with these children being shot in the streets," said Johnson. Johnson added, "And the police, Black or otherwise, should definitely be the most vocal in taking the lead in opposing such barbaric police actions."

Lessons Learned

We have come full circle as we are now faced with the same circumstances we were grappling with in 1972. We have the benefit of having an established blueprint to review as we create a new agenda. Much of what worked then could serve us now. Re-igniting a spirit of unity and commitment may be the best point of departure. This will require some personal sacrifice on all of our parts.

If this point is not understood, what more can be said...

Cheryl Johnson
K Kelly McElroy, Cleveland Ohio

The Black Shield Police Association is developing a comprehensive history of Blacks in the Cleveland Police Department. The research and the accounts provided will be published as an historical reference book.

We want your experiences to be part of this book. Please forward your personal accounts and experiences to:

Cheryl Johnson

cherylrjohnson7@gmail.com

(216) 534-0778

And/or

K Kelly McElroy

uptownliterary@gmail.com

(216) 355-1565

We look forward to hearing from you!

THE OURSTORY INITIATIVE

The Black Shield

Police Association

Black Shield is committed to do its part in making our community better. Initiatives like minority police recruitment, are still ongoing and the fight for civil justice and equality are on-going.

We are also supporting initiatives that promote education and literary excellence. We thank all of the members of Black Shield and those in the community-at-large for your support of these efforts.

COMMUNITY INVOLVEMENT

The Black Shield Police Association

The Black Shield Police Association
In conjunction with
The Office Of U.S. Senator Sherrod Brown D-OH
Present
Public Safety Minority Recruit Fair

October 3, 2015

12:00 PM - 3:00 PM
Cuyahoga Community College
(Metro Campus)
2500 E.22nd St
Jerry Sue Thornton Bldg. #194
Cleveland, Ohio 44115

FREE EVENT!

Sign up for Pre-civil service training for Police, Fire, EMS

For More Info Contact: Black Shield Police Association
President Lynn Hampton 216-323-6155

OUR YOUNG VOICES IS A PRIDE IN AUTHORSHIP INITIA-
TIVE PUBLICATION. THE YOUNG AUTHORS SELECTED
HAVE SUCCESSFULLY CONVEYED THEIR THOUGHTS,
DREAMS, AND CONCERNS BY THE WRITTEN WORD.
THEY DESERVE TO BE CELEBRATED!

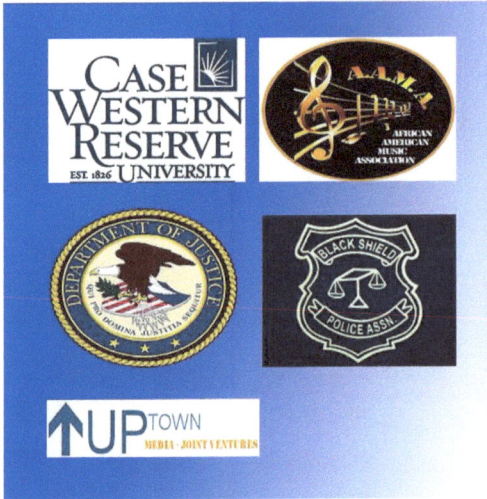

OUR YOUNG VOICES™

**2016
Cleveland, Ohio Chapter
Scholarship Week**
*Banquet
College Fair
Our Young Voices Dream Contest*

Our

Journey

Past, Present, Future

UP TOWN
MEDIA JOINT VENTURES
PUBLISHING

The Journey Continues...